50 THINGS TO KNOW
BOOK SERIES
REVIEWS FROM READERS

I recently downloaded a couple of books from this series to read over the weekend thinking I would read just one or two. However, I so loved the books that I read all the six books I had downloaded in one go and ended up downloading a few more today. Written by different authors, the books offer practical advice on how you can perform or achieve certain goals in life, which in this case is how to have a better life.

The information is simple to digest and learn from, and is incredibly useful. There are also resources listed at the end of the book that you can use to get more information.

50 Things To Know To Have A Better Life: Self-Improvement Made Easy! by Dannii Cohen

---

This book is very helpful and provides simple tips on how to improve your everyday life. I found it to be useful in improving my overall attitude.

50 Things to Know For Your Mindfulness & Meditation Journey by Nina Edmondso

---

Quick read with 50 short and easy tips for what to think about before starting to homeschool.

50 Things to Know

50 Things to Know About Getting Started with Homeschool by Amanda Walton

I really enjoyed the voice of the narrator, she speaks in a soothing tone. The book is a really great reminder of things we might have known we could do during stressful times, but forgot over the years.

- HarmonyHawaii

50 Things to Know to Manage Your Stress: Relieve The Pressure and Return The Joy To Your Life

by Diane Whitbeck

There is so much waste in our society today. Everyone should be forced to read this book. I know I am passing it on to my family.

50 Things to Know to Downsize Your Life: How To Downsize, Organize, And Get Back to Basics

by Lisa Rusczyk Ed. D.

Great book to get you motivated and understand why you may be losing motivation. Great for that person who wants to start getting healthy, or just for you when you need motivation while having an established workout routine.

50 Things To Know To Stick With A Workout: Motivational Tips To Start The New You Today

by Sarah Hughes

50 THINGS TO KNOW ABOUT SEARCH ENGINE OPTIMIZATION

THE GUIDE FOR BEGINNERS

Kiran Shahzadi

50 Things to Know

Cover designed by: Ivana Stamenkovic
Cover Image: https://pixabay.com/en/modern-analyst-marketing-bluetooth-
1316900/

CZYK Publishing Since 2011.

50 Things to Know
Visit our website at www.50thingstoknow..com

Lock Haven, PA
All rights reserved.

ISBN: 9781723980718

50 THINGS TO KNOW ABOUT SEARCH ENGINE OPTIMIZATION

50 Things to Know

BOOK DESCRIPTION

Do you want to know what Search Engine Optimization is?

Do you want to make your website user-friendly?

Would you like some guidance on how to optimize your website?

If you answered yes to any of these questions then this book is for you...

50 Things to Know about Search Engine Optimization by Kiran Shahzadi offers an approach to search engine optimization in an easy process for all the beginners. Most books on SEO tell you how to optimize your website in a search engine friendly manner using different techniques. Although there's nothing wrong with that, by reading 50 Things to Know about Search Engine Optimization, you will be able to understand how search engines crawl and index a website and how you will be able to optimize your website according to Google updates. Based on knowledge from the world's leading experts like Rand Fishkin, Brian Dean, Spencer Haws, and many

more, the book will give you the advanced knowledge of SEO, and how to delve deeper and do all the dirty work to rank a highly competitive keyword with the advanced tools.

In these pages, you'll discover all about recent SEO updates and its process. This book will help you to understand the technicalities of today's Search Engine Optimization and how to stay updated about search engines updates.

By the time you finish this book, you will be able to understand the technicalities of SEO and know how to optimize your website in a search engine friendly manner. So grab YOUR copy today. You'll be glad you did.

TABLE OF CONTENTS

DEDICATION

This book is dedicated to each person who is passionate about Search Engine Optimization. As a newbie to this field, this book will help you every time you get confused.

And to my parents, Siblings, and friends who helped me in every up and down of my life. They are my real inspiration. Especially my Father who is my hero and stands with me in every difficult situation. Thank you, Baba.

50 Things to Know

ABOUT THE AUTHOR

Kiran Shahzadi is a Graduate from Punjab University, Lahore. She chooses to start her career in the field of Digital Marketing. The world of the internet was always her passion. She always wondered how Google works and provides the accurate information to the users. How do simple business graduates understand the technicalities of search engines operations? Right!!

When she entered the world of Digital Marketing, she felt intimidated by the many terms and process of Search Engine Optimization But her passion leads her to the place where she is today. She is still in the process of learning and making her way slowly and progressively in this field.

She is currently providing her services as a freelancer in the field of Digital Marketing and providing her services as an SEO expert and Content Writer.

Where you find her on social media:
https://www.facebook.com/kiran.shahzadi26
www.twitter.com/ @Shahzadi26Kiran

50 Things to Know

INTRODUCTION

*"...The SEO's job today is more
than keywords and backlinks. It's
more than metadata optimisation.
It's more than even content. It's the
assurance of frictionless user
experience while delivering the
right information at the right time –
and in the timely manner."*

Dainius Runkevicius

The most important question in today's Digital Marketing is, what Search Engine Optimization actually is? Is it making your website friendly to search engines or is it to offer the content to the user in an SEO format? Or is it to gain more traffic to your website?

We have to go into details to understand all the technicalities of SEO. We have to learn how search engines; Google, Yahoo, and Bing operate. When you entered the world of Digital Marketing, you have to learn a lot of concepts and may feel intimidated by the sheer volume of it. Once you entered the world, prepare yourself for the constant process of learning.

There are many SEO Guru like Brain Dean, Neil Patel, and Rand Fishkin who are in this field for more than a decade, but they have to learn many things because Google is updating constantly.

If you are planning to build a website or create a blog of your own, you have to learn every tip and trick involved in the process. It will help you optimize your website and generate more traffic and create a brand awareness of your business across the globe. Once you learn all the components, you will need to play catch-up on all the strategies and tactics of the search engine.

Now the question is why search engine optimization is necessary? The answer to the question is SEO make it easier to understand the data of your website to search engines robot and users. It helps the search engines what each page is about and how it will be useful for the user. To state it easier, SEO makes your website both, user and search engine friendly.

A brief history of search engine optimization

I am not going to get you all bored by the long history of search engine optimization. ☺ I will just explain the major updates of SEO since its birth in the mid 90's.

In the mid 90's there is the excessive use of keywords, tagging and spammy backlinks to get high on search results.

In 2005, Google plays a major role in providing more relevant and authentic content to its user. The search engine brought many changes in that time period and penalizes the websites which used spammy backlinks and keyword stuffing to rank higher. The birth of local SEO is in the same time period, which helps the user with relevant and more valuable information near them.

In 2008, Google launched different tools like Google suggest, Keyword Planner Tool, Google Analytics, and Google Trends which made the optimization easier and more focused.

In 2012, the major updates from Google have restricted the websites to more focus on the keyword usage, content quality and over optimization. In that time, social media become the mainstream of SEO and Google introduces Google + with the +1 button, which played a significant role in the content visibility.

Modern-Age: In modern times mobile plays a vital role in the search engine optimization. The websites which are not optimized according to the mobile devices have lost their significance in Google search. The website needs to be mobile friendly because the user experience has been changed and Google follow the trends to improve the user experience. Nowadays, you can optimize your website by building quality links, long-tail keywords, and quality content.

The Future: The internet is changing rapidly to give a more personalize and user-friendly experience. SEO will continue to develop gradually to give the user a more niche-focused high-quality and unique content. Prepare your website for these changes to develop a strong, consistent presence and keep up social influence on the search engines.

1. SEARCH ENGINES; HOW THEY OPERATE

Well, a person who is not related to the field of Information Technology can have an idea what search engines are but how they operate? A blank space…..

When you entered the world of the World Wide Web to start your search, you need an answer to your questions. Search engines are the service offered by the World Wide Web to answer the questions of internet users by entering their keyword. The most popular search engines are:

- Google
- Yahoo
- Bing

Now the question is how they operate?

Most search engines work by crawling and indexing a web page. Each web page is a unique stop for them. They need a way to crawl an entire website and find all the stops along the way by linking. Linking process allows search engines spiders or crawlers to reach the millions and millions of interconnected web pages. Then search engines provide with a ranked list of the web pages according to the user interest. Search engines assumed that the more popular a web page, website or document, the more valuable information it must contain.

2. STAY ALERTS TO GOOGLE UPDATES

In search engine optimization, you should always stay alert to the Google updates. As described in the brief history above, Google is constantly updating its algorithm to provide its user with more relevant and authentic information. The major changes so far.

Google Panda: The update in 2011 allows the search filter to stop sites that are providing low quality content and ranked higher on search results by keyword stuffing.

Google Penguin: The Penguin update in 2012 allowed Google to tackle all the websites which are using black hat SEO techniques such as link farming, and inappropriate use of Anchor Text.

Google Hummingbird: The update release in 2013 is a more comprehensive search algorithm which is more focused on the meaning and intention of the question asked by the user. It is focused on what user really wants by typing a query.

Apart from these are the major changes, Google is now more focused on a mobile-friendly website. Its focus is on app indexing, as Google announced the mobile-friendly ranking algorithm. You can stay updated by subscribing the search engine Journal and search engine land forums.

3. CONTENT MANAGEMENT SYSTEM (CMS)

A content management system is a software application that is used to create, manage and organized all your digital content. The CMS takes care of the backend coding of a website. Any business can create, edit, and publish its content by using the CMS. Although there are many other types available like Joomla, Drupal, Express Engine or a custom website, WordPress, Shopify, and Weebly are the most popular CMS which are used to publish content.

There are several benefits of using a Content Management System such as it is very easy to use and cost-effective. It reduces the website maintenance cost and doesn't let you rely on webmaster or developer for an update in the content. Optimization of the content is very easy and you can make your website mobile friendly without any hindrance.

4. ON-PAGE SEO

On-Page SEO is the process of doing search engine optimization while remaining on the website system. It is the process of doing all the technical changes to optimize the website search engine rankings. From keyword research to the site speed optimization all the process is called on-page SEO. It includes the process of keyword optimization in a web page, Meta tags optimization, the process of crawling and submitting your website to search engine, the use of Google webmaster tool, adding robot and submitting sitemaps of a website and last but not the least page loading speed of a website. The internal linking is also a part of on-page SEO.

5. OFF-PAGE SEO

Search engine optimization can be divided into two parts; On-page and Off-page SEO. Both are very important strategies for the optimization of a website. You cannot complete the process of optimization of a website without any strategy. Off-page optimization can be described as the process of link building techniques. The more external links a website has the more its domain authority. As search engines consider the website authentic one if it has the more authentic external linking. Link building process involves submitting your website to high domain authority websites. There are certain techniques to create links like directory submission, web2.0 links, article submission, guest posting, social bookmarking, image sharing, video sharing and many more. The Off-page technique is widely used by the experts to generate more traffic to your website.

6. KEYWORD RESEARCH

We have discussed what search engines are and how they work? Now let's delve deeper and discussed the main part which is how to do search engine optimization? Well, search engine optimization starts with keyword research. A keyword is a specific term in your website content that made it possible for people to find you on search engines. For example, if you type "how to do SEO in 2018". Then the result showings are the websites that are giving information about SEO. Thus the keyword, in this case, is "SEO".

Now where to find the keywords which are the less competitive and showing more monthly researches for a specific term? There is a full procedure to find the perfect keyword. You need to start with a seed word for your niche. Type the seed word in Google and see what related searches are showing for that word at the end of the page. Seoquake is a Google extension which is also helpful in finding the keyword. It is a must-have tool for every SEO expert. You can find the exact and related keyword data with seoquake extension by typing in your Google search bar "keyword" and Allintitle:keyword.

7. KEYWORD.IO

"Keyword.io" is a free tool to generate more keywords from your seed keyword. You can generate the keyword ideas by just sign up. It can give you a range of long tail keywords ideas that can rank your website. It uses the data of Google autocomplete search predictions. It can generate up to 750 keyword suggestions with some excellent long tail keywords. The tool enables you to export a CSV file containing all the keyword ideas and showing the results like Monthly searches worldwide, Monthly searches local, Competitiveness, Average CPC, Monthly traffic volume you receive, Related landing pages you search. Based on these results, you can choose the keyword in which you want to rank your website.

8. GOOGLE ADWORD KEYWORD PLANNER TOOL

Now the main part of keyword research is Google Adwords keyword planner tool. This tool is also free and easy to use. Sign in with your g-mail account and use the filters to find the exact and relevant data. It will show you the result like CPC, Average monthly searches, keyword usage, and difficulty etcetera. If you use all these tools to find the keyword then you will find the right keyword to get ranked on Google for your website. This tool allows you to find the exact and relevant keyword and beneficial to both your business and/or potential customers. The tools also show you how to spend your budget on a campaign while finding the right keyword for your business.

How does the tool work?

When you describe your term in Google keyword planner tool, the people might be searching for many variations and combination for that term. But you don't have to bid for many terms or keywords related to your business. As I mentioned above to use filters to know what your potential customers are looking for. The target filters may help you find whether the keyword is popular in your area or not. You can target the location, language, search network, and negative keywords by using filters and know what the people in your areas are looking for. The Google Adword keyword planner tool is cost effective and easy to use.

9. MARKET SAMURAI

The tool Market Samurai is very popular for researching the targeted keyword related to your niche. It is a paid tool with a 12-day free trial. The software is downloadable and you have to install it on your PC. Make sure you have Adobe Air and Adobe Flash Player installed in your computer. The features included in this program are Keyword Research, SEO competition, Find content, Monetization, Publish Content, Promotions, and Domains. As in Google Adwords account, you have to use filters in Market Samurai to get the exact data related to your keyword.

10. LSI KEYWORDS GRAPH

In Search Engine Optimization Keyword is the main key to rank a website that's why keyword research is so systemized and important in SEO. LSI words can make the old content a new one and help you to improve your ranking and create more visibility in search engines. The term LSI means Latent Semantic Indexing, a method search engines used to study and compare the different terms and their relationship. The LSI keywords are the highlighted words related to your keyword when you search. It is a free tool and works like "Keyword.io" tool. Just type your keyword in the search bar area and it will give you different related keywords.

LSI keywords are used to boost your SEO ranking. You can use LSI word in your Meta Description. Use the main keyword and 2-3 LSI words in your content. Generate most relevant word related to your keyword by LSI graph. Use LSI words in your PPC campaigns. Use LSI keywords for the image optimization of an old image.

11. CONTENT WRITING

Now we have the perfect keyword for a website by using all the above-mentioned method. What to do with the keyword? Well, the next step is to write a unique content to describe the services of your business. Each page of a website will need a separate keyword and a different content. While writing content for a website you should know certain rules which can be described as follows; start your content writing using the keyword you researched. Never stuff your keyword in the content as Google will penalize those who use keyword stuffing techniques. Give something informative to the reader. The content can be interlinked to the other pages of your website. Also, make your content hyperlinked when you used another website content. Keep your paragraph short, maximum 3-5 sentences in a paragraph. Use pictures in your content. Website using pictures grasp more attention of a reader. Make sure you have a legal right to that picture. Make sure your content is not plagiarized and free of any grammatical and spelling mistakes. Keep your tone simple and never complicate the sentence by using difficult words. You can use bullet points to highlight your content.

12. SEO CONTENT

In website optimization, content optimization is the most important thing. As it has the keyword for which you are ranked at different search engines. Don't put your efforts in vain by a bad optimization of the content. Well, the optimization process is easy. Just make sure you have followed these steps; Use the keyword in the main title. Use the keyword in the first paragraph of the content. It will be more beneficial if it is used in the first sentence. Use your keyword in H1 of your content. (H1 stands for the headings of the content). If the content has (H2) subheadings then make sure to use the keyword in at least one of the subheadings. Use your keyword in describing the picture you have added in the content.

13. IMAGE ALT TEXT

One important thing is that Google cannot read the images. Image alt tags are the HTML attributes applied to the images for search engines to read the images. You can optimize your website with images optimization also. If you are running an e-com store then image optimization is plus point for your business. Google bots and search engines crawl an image with its alt tags attribute and know how the page is indexed and what its rankings are. It is also useful for the user of a webpage, as he/she can understand the content easily. You can recognize an alt tag attribute of an image by:

<img src="image.png"alt="image_alt_attribute"/>

For images SEO you have to; Make sure you have compressed all the images of your webpage, as it will affect your website speed. Keep alt attribute short and simple and add your keyword. Make sure to not use the keyword stuffing technique, as it is negative SEO. Also, do not use alt tags over the title of the image.

14. SEO FRIENDLY URL

SEO friendly URL is the most neglected issue while considering on-page optimization. Google pays attention to the websites whose URL structure is SEO friendly. Now, what should be the URL structure of the website? The structure of a website URL should be understandable both by the Google bots and user and not in numeric format. While structuring the URL of a website you should follow the following instructions; The URL structure of your site should be readable by the human beings. Use your keyword in the URL. It should be a short minimum 50 to 60 characters. Do not use characters in URL such as &, @, %, $, etc. as it will be difficult for Google to crawl the website. Do not uses stop words in the URL. Do not stuff your keyword in the URL. Use the hyphen instead of spaces. For example,

www.example.com/how-to-do-search-engine-optimization.html

Some example of bad URL's are:

www.exaample.com/seo%friendly%URL.html

www.example.com/news.html#latest

www.example.com/product.aspx?ID=22536&T=3

fg65

15. META TAGS

Meta tags play an important role in the search engine optimization as it represents your webpage on Google. We can say that it is a kind of advertisement for your website. Meta tags do not display on the webpage but they appear in the page code exist in HTML and appear usually at the head of a page. Meta tags are only visible to search engines. To improve your rankings on the search engines, you should use them in the best possible way. If you have not written a Meta description of your webpage, then Google automatically generate a Meta description based on the content. But it is a bad practice for your SEO.

There are three important elements in the Meta tags:

1. Meta title
2. Meta description
3. URL

As we already discussed what should be the structure of a website URL. We should focus on the other two factors; Meta title and description here. Meta title is the title of a webpage in Google search snippet. Each webpage has its own title. A short description of the content in a webpage is called Meta description. Like the title, each webpage has its own Meta description. While writing the Meta title and description you have to keep in mind the following things; Use your keyword in the Meta title and description. The length of the title should be 50-60 characters (5 to 7 words). The length of the Meta description is 150-160 characters (30-45 words). Always follow the Google updates. As in 2017, the length of the Meta description is 320 characters but in 2018, it is back to 160 characters.

16. GOOGLE ANALYTICS

Google Analytics is a free tool provided by Google to track and analyze your website statistics. It is the most popular digital analytics software among the digital marketers. The tools give the detailed information about the traffic of your website. It will give the information like; who visits your website? When they visit? What is the time? What is the geographical location of the visitor? What are the pages they visit?

It will also allow you to see which social media refer to your website and which content of your website shared the most. It will give a detailed report of the content analysis of your website. Google Analytics tool can be easily integrated with other tools. It can give you fantastic results when it works with Google AdWords account. It will give you the useful insights that will lead you to the success of your AdWords campaigns. The Analytics tool also helps you to find why visitors are bouncing off your site.

Now how to use Google Analytics? Type Google Analytics in your Google search bar, open the website and create a free account if you don't have a Google account. If you have, just sign in with Google account. Set a property in your Analytics account by adding your website. Go to Account level, create a new account then select your website URL, the relevant category of site, local zone, target area, and terms and services. Get the tracking ID of your website.

Go to your website admin panel; paste the tracking code into your website header section. If you have a WordPress website then use plugin Google Analytics. Save changes. You can customize your reports on the basis of provided data.

17. GOOGLE WEBMASTER TOOL/ SEARCH CONSOLE

As the name describes, Google Webmaster tool is a set of tool for all the webmasters to check the different aspects of your website. It is helpful for a website in finding; How Google sees your website. Which internal and external links appear on your website? To adjust the crawl rate at which Google bots index your website. Check the keyword user type who land on your webpage. Check the click-through rate of the keyword. Statistics of your website and many more.

If the Webmaster tool collaborates with other Google Tool like Google Analytics, it will show you even better results. Google Webmaster tool is a very powerful tool in SEO and easy to use. Like every other tool provided by Google, it is also free. There are several sections in its dashboard and you have access to all of these important sections including;

Search queries: It will show you the result of the keyword that the user used and land on your webpage.

Links: Here you can see the report of all external and internal backlinks that are linked to your website.

Crawl errors: This section shows you the crawl errors Google bot encountered on your website.

Keywords: The keyword section shows you which keyword Google finds significant on your site.

Sitemap: You can control your sitemaps in this section. It will show you how many sitemaps Google found on your site and also the number of URL in them.

These tools give you the information about your website. Go to Google Webmaster tools, if you have a Google account then just sign in with your account. Add your website to make sure you have added both versions of your website. Google will consider it as two separate websites. For example:

https://www.example.com

https://exapmle.com

Whenever you add your website the tool will ask you to verify your website by using one of the following methods: Alternative method, Recommended, HTML tags. You can copy the code and paste it into your website. It will verify your website.

18. BING WEBMASTER TOOL

Use Bing Webmaster tool if you want your website to crawl by Bing. It is the same as the Google webmaster tool. You have to submit your website in Bing search engine. It provides a user-friendly interface which allows you to handle multiple sites with a single account. It will give you the information like clicks, impression, pages indexed and pages crawled, etcetera. First, you have to verify your site and submit the code in your website. Site dashboard allows you to see all the recent activity including all sitemaps you have submitted, your top keyword researches, and all inbound links.

The tools like configure my site, the sitemap is easy to use in Bing Webmaster tool. It also supports the video extension through XML sitemap to index your videos. The features like submit URL, ignore URL parameter, crawl control setting, deep links, block URL's make it popular among the digital marketers. You can customize your report related to keywords research, SEO report, inbound links report, crawl-information report, and page traffic report. Bing Webmaster tool gives you the certain diagnostic tool to fix all your website errors. It also gives tools

like keyword research tool, link explorer, fetches as
Bing bot, verifies the Bing bot tool, SEO Analyzer.
Just like the Google Webmaster tool, add your
website in both www and non-www version. And
copy the copy provided by the Bing webmaster and
paste it to your website. It gives you three options for
submitting the code. Meta Tags verification allows
you to verify by inserting a custom line of code
provided by Bing into your website Home page.
"BingSiteAuth.xml": it is downloadable file and
needs to be submitted into your website route code.
DNS verification requires a bit technical assistance in
the verification process. To submit your verification
code you will need access to your hosting to edit
CNAME record.

19. ROBOTS.TXT

Robots are also important when you consider
Search engine optimization. Robot.txt is the file
which you are asking search engines to disallow. You
need to be careful when you are editing your robot.txt
file because you can harm your business if you are
not careful. The file created by the webmasters to

allow web robots to crawl the web pages. Robot.txt files allow you to block the development related files, comments section, negative keyword, and spam feedbacks.

The usual structure of Robot.txt file is:

User-agent:*

Disallow: /wp-admin/ (if it is a WordPress site)

Disallow: /cgi-bin/

Disallow: /comments/

Disallow: /search/

Disallow: /trackbacks/

You can add words like Disallow, Allow, Crawls, and Delays in the robot.txt file. The file can disallow or allow any commands which are given to them. The Robot.txt files are so important that it can affect your presence in SERP. You need to take a look at all the directories that you want to Disallow like cgi-bin, wp-admin, script, carts and others that contain important data. Make sure you have disallowed the duplicate content to index by search engines. Also, make sure that search engines indexed the important content of your website. You can avoid search engines rankings problems by ensuring the proper use of robot.txt files.

20. SITEMAP.XML

Sitemaps are the XML files which contain all the URLs of your webpage. These XML files should be easily recognizable by Google bots to crawl. Sitemaps are used for search engines to crawl the web pages so that nothing important can be missed in a page. You can create a sitemap easily. You can add sitemaps by using Google Webmaster tool dashboard. Go to crawl → sitemaps→ add sitemaps.

You can generate sitemaps of your web pages with any sitemap generator tool. But if you have a WordPress website, Yoast SEO plugin allows you to create a sitemap of your webpage automatically. Go to Yost SEO → features →xml sitemaps and activate it. The structure of a sitemap is:

www.site.com/sitemap_index.xml

The search engine sees all the pages you want to index. The more pages you index the more trust your website gains. It means that you have more information to give to the user.

21. SITE SPEED OPTIMIZATION

Search engines also consider your website speed as a process of optimization. Your website needs to mobile and desktop friendly. Google consider website speed as a ranking factor. In a recent update, the mobile site loading speed also matters. A fast website speed leads to a good user experience (UX) and a good user experience can convert the leads for your business. The minimum site loading speed is 2-3 seconds in Google. Because of high competition, your website speed needs to load within 2-3 seconds. If not then Google will consider other sites and rank them higher than yours. If a web page load in more than 10 seconds then it will be a negative ranking factor.

Now the question is how to check your website speed and speed up your website? Well, there are certain tools through which you can check your website score both mobile and desktop. The tools also give you the solutions for how to speed up your site. The tools used to check the website speeds are:

1. Page speed insights
2. Pingdom website speed test
3. GT matrix

These are the well-known tools which are used to asssess the website speed. Just type the tool in Google open website and copy and paste your website link, Enter and boom. Here are the results showing the factors that are slowing your website speed. The most common errors affecting the speed of a website are; leverage browsing cache, image optimization, image compression, CSS minification, and JavaScript minification, etcetera. By solving these issues you can optimize your website speed.

22. YOAST SEO

Yoast SEO is a WordPress plugin used to optimize the web page content in a search engine friendly way. The plugin is very popular among the SEO experts and used widely. It is available in both free and premium version. The free version gives you feature like keyword optimization, the preview of your page in Google, Facebook, and Twitter, Readability check, full control over breadcrumbs, no duplicate content, technical stuff in the background, and always updated for Google algorithm. While the premium version gives you the all the above feature plus internal linking suggestion, content insights, redirect managers, focus keyword export, 1-year free access to 27/7 support. The premium version is ad-free while in the free version you will get ads of WordPress other products and services.

When you enter the focus keyword, Yoast SEO plugin allows you to see all the problems, improvements, good result of a webpage. You can easily optimize your webpage by following the instruction given in the problems and improvement section. The snippet preview shows you the result of how your webpage will appear on Google when someone searches for that keyword. In the snippet preview, you can easily add the Meta title and Meta description according to Google updates. The readability analysis shows the exact content analysis of your web pages. It will analyze the heading, subheadings, paragraph length, sentence length, and the tone of your content and passive voice alerts as Google does not like passive voice sentences. It also provides you with the webmaster or search console feature through which you can verify the code and allow Google Webmaster to crawl your web pages. We can say that Yoast SEO plugin is a very supportive tool in search engine optimization but the

only disadvantage is that it is only available for a
WordPress website.

23. ALL IN ONE SEO TOOL

Like Yoast SEO, All in One SEO tool is also
popular among the digital marketers. You can use all
in one SEO tool instead of Yoast SEO. The features
are almost the same of both tools but there are some
distinctions also. The plugin is also for WordPress
website only. All in one SEO allows you to improve
your SEO like Meta tags, generate sitemaps and avoid
the duplicate contents of your website in an easy
interface using the WordPress dashboard. It is also
available in both free and premium version. The
premium version has some more features like video
sitemaps, e-com SEO, 1-year support and many more.
The All in one SEO tool allow set up your home page
Meta's, it enables all in one pack for your content to
both your posts and pages. It can help you with your
Google Analytics account. It helps you to add Meta's
to all content of your website and last but not the least
it helps you to generate eth sitemaps of your web
pages. It has all the settings in a single page and

easier and faster to use. Help icon is next to each setting thus it is easy to use.

24. LOCAL SEO/NAP

As described above, search engines are considering local searches in the recent updates. It is very important for small businesses as four out of five people use the search engines for local product information. If you want your business to work online, then it is necessary for you to do local SEO or NAP. NAP means Name, Address, and Phone Number of your business. If you have a small business and you want to rank in search engines for organic local search results, then NAP is very necessary. In local search optimization, you need to constantly update your website, add your business in Google directory through Google my business tool. Google my business is a tool offered by Google to help your business online needs. You need to create and verify an account on it.

Now, what is the process of local SEO? How to add NAP in your Google my business account? The process involves 4 important steps geo sitemap, locations.kml, H-card, and Microdata schema.

You can add geositemap by going to the geositemap generator. In the open window add a name, address, city, state, zip code, country, and description. Always make you have the same information added to your website. Because Google and other search engines make sure through another web that you are using the same business address. The next step is to download your location.kml and geositemap. Upload these files to your website and add geositemap to your search console for crawling. Make sure you have added sitemap for both www and non-www versions.

25. SEOQUAKE

Seoquake is a very effective and a must-have tool in search engine optimization. It is a Google extension available on all type of browsers like Chrome and Firefox and also available on ios (iPad & iPhone). It is free and easy to use. It can give you the SEO analysis data of any website without any cost. You can download the extension in any browser you use. The installation process is easy. Once installed it will give you the data related to the keyword you typed in the Google search bar and all the competitor analysis of that keyword. Click the sq button on the upper right corner of your chrome browser and it will give you all the data like the website Alexa rank, Google index, Bing index, semrush analysis, the domain analysis and the total backlinks of a website.

It will also give you the full report of a webpage internal and external linking and provides you the data about no-follow and do-follow backlinks. By clicking the Diagnosis tab you are able to find all the factors which are affecting your website SEO. The new feature traffic analysis is a powerful feature when combined with the semrush free account. It will give you the advance backlink report and all the Google updates in your Google search console directly. We can say that it is a one pack powerful suit.

26. MOZ OPEN SITE EXPLORER/ LINK EXPLORER

Moz open site explorer is a powerful tool when you consider the off page techniques and want to find your competitors backlinks. The Link explorer let you uncover your competitor's backlinks, create your strategy and track your progress. The Moz open site explorer is available in free and premium version. The limitation in the free version is to check 10 queries per month. With 4.8 trillion pages recovered, 53 million root domain and 25 trillion links it can lead you to powerful link building. Open the link explorer and paste your website link, press enter. You'll see domain authority, link domains, inbound links, and ranking keywords. You can download all the reports in a CSV file. To keep a track of your online marketing campaign, you can track the lost and discovered links in the last 60 days. In the top metrics section, you will get an overview of top links of your site, top pages of your website and also find the anchor text which is most followed on your website.

You can get the several content ideas with Moz link explorer tool. You can use all the above mention report to create a content strategy for your website. You can check your competitor's backlinks techniques by checking it on link explorer. Also, check from the top pages result in their content techniques and try to adopt them. Check what backlinks which they have lost and try to achieve them. You can also easily analyze your competitor's keyword strategy.

27. SMALL SEO TOOLS

Small SEO tool is a website full of a set of tools that offers you free help in the optimization. It has the fastest and accurate tools to edit and create content for your website. Its purpose is to check your content for search engine optimization, grammatical mistakes, and also compare it with other website contents for plagiarism purpose. The set of tools available at the small SEO tools website are; text content tools, images editing tools, keywords tools, backlinks tools, website management tools, website tracking tools, proxy tools, domain tools, meta tags tools, password management tools, and online PDF tools.

Although the most popular one among these are; plagiarism checker, grammar checker, spells checker, word count checker, article re-writer/spinner, backlinks checker, backlinks maker, keyword density checker, keyword position checker, domain authority checker, page authority checker, domain age checker, mozrank checker and website SEO score checker. If you want to create a blog of your own, then you should consider smallseotools.com as it is totally free and can give you the more relevant results related to your queries. It helps not only bloggers but also SEO experts, social media entrepreneur, and website owners in creating plagiarism and grammatical free content.

28. COST PER CLICK (CPC) /PAY PER CLICK (PPC)

CPC is the cost of each Adwords campaign you want to start or already started. Pay per click is each payment of an ad when someone clicks on your ad showing in the Google search snippet. The PPC campaign is more effective when it compares to CPC. The major benefit of PPC is the immediate traffic to your website when someone clicks. But it requires for you to think strategically and create a successful PPC campaign. Use Adwords research carefully. To check the demand for keywords uses the tools. Organize your keywords. You should run a campaign while considering your budget. And last but not the least don't forget to check your competitor's keywords and successful campaigns by using Moz link explorer.

29. AFFILIATE MARKETING

If you are a blogger and have a high traffic on your blog, then you should have a good knowledge of Affiliate marketing. In simple words, Affiliate marketing is the process of writing an article about some product and describes the specification and when someone buys the product by reading your blog you will get a commission. Most of the bloggers out there are using affiliate marketing to earn money. The commission can be $1 or $10,000 based on the product. The company gives you a unique tracking URL by which they can track a certain blogger who gains the lead. There are several companies which are selling their products online. By signing up with them you can get the unique tracking ID and can write the products specifications.

30. BACKLINKS

Backlinks are the off-page SEO techniques used to generate traffic to your website. The more backlinks, the more a website has credibility on search engines. There are different techniques used to create the high-quality backlinks. You need to decide on a proper strategy for the backlinks purpose. Make sure that you have a high quality and consistent content. Try to give quotes and interviews in your backlinks. You need to build a strong social media presence to increase backlinks. A consistency presence at blogs and forums may help you generate traffic to your site. Make sure you have connected to the right people who have an interest in your niche. Try to guest post in some high-quality websites. Always monitor your backlinks. The use of video and images is common in the off-page strategy.

31. WEB 2.0

Web 2.0 is the most popular backlinks generating technique used by SEO experts. You have to use only white hat SEO techniques to create web 2.0 backlinks. Do not try to get spammy backlinks by keyword stuffing techniques. You need to be careful about creating web 2.0 backlinks. Always complete your profile. Try to make your appearance as a brand in your social profiles. You can create blog pages like Tumblr, WordPress, YouTube, Blogspot, Facebook, and Instagram pages for a high profile backlinks. Publish original content on these blogs. After Google updates, many of you would think does Google consider web 2.0 as a backlink? The answer is yes, Google still considers web 2.0 a strong backlink if used as white hat SEO. The best part is you can have as many web 2.0 backlinks as you want.

32. SOCIAL BOOKMARKING

Social Bookmarking is another backlink technique widely used by digital marketers. It is a way to bookmark your web pages on different social sites. The bookmarks are public and can be viewed by other members of the site. It is also called social indexing, social tagging, collaborative tagging, and folksonomy. If you stay active on the social bookmarking sites like Digg and Del.icio.us then it will get a new opportunity for traffic to your website. It can lead your website to be shared by people through tagging. If you add the social bookmarking button to your website, it will increase the traffic to your site. It also helps you to create your personal branding awareness. All you need to do is register with the social bookmarking site. The social bookmarking sites are free to use. Some of bookmarking sites are Tumblr, Reddit, Facebook, Twitter, Stumbleupon, Diggo, Digg, and Pinterest.

33. DIRECTORY SUBMISSION

Directory submission is also of the most popular way to get backlinks from web directories. It is used to increase rankings in the search engine and SERP's. It is the process of submitting your website or blog in the relevant category with some details. You can submit your website in three different ways; free listing, paid listing, and reciprocal listing. In the free listing, you can submit your website to any web directory without any cost but it may take some time to list your link. You can get as many high-quality backlinks you want. If you want instant directory submission then you should choose the paid one method. In reciprocal you have to submit directories with the link of web directory on your website. You have to add a Title, website URL, a short description of a minimum 100 words, and e-mail ID.

34. BROKEN LINKS

If someone visits your website and find it unresponsive because of broken backlink, then it will create a bad user experience. Broken links are bad user experience in the eye of search engines. You are making so many efforts in creating the quality backlinks but if they are not working then it will create a negative score on your SEO efforts. You need to check periodically your website for any broken link and fix them. There are several tools to find the broken links i.e. Google Analytics and Xenu. Check your broken links by using Google Analytics and Xenu tools and make a report of all the links. In the next step organize your backlinks report and analyze the data and decide which page should be redirected. After identifying the pages, go to your website CMS and redirect your web pages.

35. RECIPROCAL LINKS

Reciprocal links mean you need to give backlink to another website in exchange for a backlink to increase traffic to your website. This technique is called a link scheme and is not consider as white hat SEO technique. It violates the Google webmaster guidelines. For example, if a website has a reciprocal link despite irrelevancy of content to each other site. Then Google will consider it a bad backlink and it will affect your website ranking.

36. PAGE SPEED INSIGHTS

Page Speed Insights is a tool by Google which provides a detailed analysis of your website performance on both mobile and desktop and tell you how to improve its performance. After the full on-page and off-page SEO, you need to have a periodical analysis of your website by Page Speed Insights and check your website performance. If your website responding time is not quick then you will surely lose your traffic. Copy and paste your website URL in the search bar and analyze your website. The score point is 0 to 100, 85 and above means your website performance is A+. If low, then you have to take action to increase your website speed. Page Speed Insights suggest you the solution how to improve website speed. By following the instructions you can boost up your speed. CSS and JavaScript minification, image compression, and optimization, and landing page redirects are the most common errors detect by the tool. Improve your website speed by solving all the errors.

37. DOMAIN AUTHORITY/ PAGE AUTHORITY

The Domain Authority is a set of score allocated by MOZ to decide how well a website is ranked on search engines. The score is from 1 to 100, the higher the best domain a website has. It is calculated by the number of backlinks and linking root domain into a single DA score. If a website has the high number of quality backlinks then its domain score will be high.

A Page Authority determines how well a web page will be ranked on Search engine result pages (SERP).

The score is 1 to 100, 1 for lowest and 100 being highest. A page authority only tells you about a web page but the Domain Authority tells you about the entire domain score. The page authority depends on links, MOZ rank, MOZ trust, and many other factors.

38. NO FOLLOW/DO FOLLOW

No follow is a tag in a backlink that does not allow search engines to follow that link. If your website has a no follow the link then search engines do not detect it with link juice. These types of links have less weight in the eye of search engines. An example of no follow link is:

<a href="https://www.example.com/"rel="nofollow">Google</a>

DoFollow links are the links allows search engines to follow them. The dofollow links have the full weight of backlinks. It will detect by the link juice of the search engines. It is a best practice for you to allow do follow the link as anchor text. It means that you are using the targeted keyword in the backlinks. Example of do follow link is:

<a href="https://www.example.com/">Google</a>

39. SERP

When you use search engines for something, the resulting pages that appear in the answer of your search are SERP. SERP stands for Search Engine Results Pages. Each SERP is unique and provides results by user location, browsing history and social settings. There are two types of results showing in the SERP; Paid and Organic. Organic results are the results which appear organically when a user enters a specific term. Search Engines Optimization specialist can optimize the web content and show their website on SERP organically. The box on the right side is Knowledge Graph introduce by Google in 2012 that pulls data from a specific term a user enter at the time of research. The paid results are the results when an advertiser pays for a certain ad to show on search engines.

40. WEB CRAWLING

Search engines use web crawler techniques to crawl website content and its pages. The web crawlers look for a specific keyword on a webpage, content on the page, and look for every link a web page has. They give this information to the search engines to go ahead further. The process is called web crawling. All the web pages are indexed by software called web crawler. It gathers the information related to each page and indexes them in the systematic and automated way. It also helps in the validation of HTML code and links attached to a web page. When a user types a keyword, these crawlers scan all the relevant web pages for that keyword or term and index them accordingly. According to Google, there are more than 60 trillion indexed web pages. Web crawler searches all these pages for the relevant information the user wants.

41. WEB INDEXING

Web indexing can be defined as the process of downloading and sorting out all the web pages on search engines. Search engines need this information because they need to give their user the most relevant results to its users. There are several methods provided by the search engine to get your web pages indexed with search engines. Submitting XML sitemaps is one of the most important ways to get your web pages indexed. By submitting XML sitemaps of each web page of your website you can get indexed. Meta Robot tags also help search engines in indexation of the web pages. Robot.txt also allows or disallows search engines to index a web page.

42. 301/302 REDIRECTS

When a user visits your website and found the error in opening page, he will get frustrated and never get back to your website. In Search Engine Optimization, error page not found is a "BIG NO". That why redirects are used to enhance both the user experience (UI) and search engines. The purpose of redirect is to send both user and search engines to another page of your website when they request a certain page and it is not available. The most common redirect used for SEO is 301 Redirects which means the page is moved permanently to the other page of the website. The use of 301 redirects is a healthy practice for Search Engine Optimization purpose. Similarly, 302 Redirect is another method which means "found" or "moved temporarily". However, it is suggested to use 301 Redirect for SEO.

43. 404 NOT FOUND

404 not found is the code of HyperText Transfer Protocol which means that the page you are trying to find is not available on their server. The message can be in different ways; 404 not found, 404 errors, the requested URL was not found on this server, and 404 page not found, etc. When Google found a page not found error, it simply deletes the page and all its data from the indexes. You will lose all the page rank which a certain page has and it will affect your page level and domain level. Most common way to remove the 404 not found error is to use 301 Redirect method.

It will help you with your website SEO and ultimately increase your domain level.

44. ANCHOR TEXT

Anchor text is any clickable hyperlink text in your content. Anchor text is the blue underlined word in the content. It can be of any color by changing the HTML code. The keyword usage in Anchor text is the way most search engines find the topic of a certain web page. It helps a specific page ranked higher on different search engines. There are several terms of Anchor text used in SEO. Targeted anchor texts are the exact keyword used to create links for SEO purpose. A backlinks anchor text is the keyword linking to another website. Excessive anchor text is the keyword stuffing technique and is a black hat SEO technique to rank your website.

45. BOUNCE RATE

A bounce rate can be defined as the percentage of visits to a certain page by the user. The higher bounce rate the low number of visitors your website going to have. The average bounce rate of a website should be 49%. A good bounce rate can be between 20-30%. The study shows that a bounce rate below 20% as it will an analytical problem and above 90%as it can be a problem with your web content, is a bad sign. You have to consider several things to improve your website bounce rate. Ensure that all the external and internal links are in proper condition. Also, make sure you are targeting the right keywords and providing the user exact answer mentioned in your Meta tags.

46. YOUTUBE SEO

The 2nd largest search engine in the world is YouTube. Many people are paying attention to the content optimization on Google, Yahoo, and Bing; But YouTube is also one of the most popular search engines for video content. You need a video to optimize your content on YouTube. Create a compelling video for your business by using different tools and get ranked for the proper keyword. Always follow the trends what people want as it will create the user engagement. Just like Google ranking you need a proper keyword research for your video. You can use keyword.io and Google Keyword Planner tool for the keyword research but make sure you have selected the YouTube Keyword suggestion tab. Use keyword in Title, Description, tags, Thumbnails, and channel name.

47. TUBEBUDDY

Tubebuddy is the Chrome extension used for the purpose of video optimization on YouTube. It provides so many features like bulk editing, direct Facebook upload, social monitoring, quick links, etc. It has all the features in its dashboard where you can access the entire monitoring tool easily. It also gives you the competitor's analysis and tells you about the keyword by which they are ranked on YouTube. Social sharing features and Thumbnail generator are also helpful in video ranking.

48. WHITE HAT SEO

White hat SEO is the strategy used to optimize the website according to search engine rules and regulations. A website using organic strategies to get visitors and use the relevant content is ranked by White hat SEO techniques. Keywords, keyword analysis, link building, backlink analysis, and creating content for the human being are some of the White hat SEO techniques. It is also called Ethical SEO and used by those people who want a long-term investment in their website.

49. BLACK HAT SEO

As the name suggests, black hat SEO is the strategy of using aggressive keyword stuffing techniques by focusing mainly on search engines. In Blackhat techniques, the guidance provided by search engines are not followed and used by those who want a quick ranking on search engines. Keyword stuffing, use of the irrelevant keyword, and invisible text are some of the black hat tactics. The result of using

black hat techniques is getting your website
permanently banned from search engines.

50. GREY HAT SEO

Grey hat SEO techniques are neither includes in
white nor black hat SEO techniques. It is risky to use
grey hat techniques as either it may rank your website
or it could cost you the loss of thousands of visitors.
One important thing to note down here is that grey hat
techniques are changing periodically. It may include
in the white or black hat in next year. The question is,
do we need to use grey hat techniques to get ranked
on Google? It is safer for you to use purely White hat
SEO tactics to get ranked on search engines.

Other Helpful Resources

Search Engine Journal
https://www.searchenginejournal.com/
Search Engine Land
https://searchengineland.com/
Baclinko by Brian Dean
https://backlinko.com/
Moz Blog
https://moz.com/google-algorithm-change

50 Things to Know

READ OTHER

50 THINGS TO KNOW

BOOKS

50 Things to Know

50 Things to Know

Website: 50thingstoknow.com

Facebook: facebook.com/50thingstoknow

Pinterest: pinterest.com/lbrennec

YouTube: youtube.com/user/50ThingsToKnow

Twitter: twitter.com/50ttk

Mailing List: Join the 50 Things to Know
Mailing List to Learn About New Releases

50 Things to Know

50 Things to Know

Please leave your honest review of this book on Amazon and Goodreads. We appreciate your positive and constructive feedback. Thank you.

50 Things to Know

.

www.ingramcontent.com/pod-product-compliance
Lightning Source LLC
Chambersburg PA
CBHW031246050326
40690CB00007B/979